Harry The High Versus Larry The Low

by Alan Champlin

atmosphere press

© 2025 Alan Champlin

Published by Atmosphere Press

No part of this book may be reproduced without permission from the author except in brief quotations and in reviews. This is a work of fiction, and any resemblance to real places, persons, or events is entirely coincidental.

Atmospherepress.com

This book is dedicated to all of those who may think that they are not "good enough" or "worthy" or are simply "different." Your uniqueness is a gift, and even if others may not appreciate it, you should! Every human being has specific talents— your goal in life should be to identify yours and use them to benefit everyone.

A special thanks to my wife, D.
Without her, this book would not be here.

I also dedicate this book to Oakley: you are special, and your story is waiting to be written.

This is possibly the most beautiful day ever. Children are laughing and playing all around.

Lots of parents are enjoying it by swimming or lounging at the pool.

Who on Earth could make such a beautiful day? Well, it's Harry the High; that's the guy!

But wait! On the horizon, the beauty is fading away. Dark clouds are rolling in quickly and the daylight seems to be disappearing.

Heavy rain is pouring, while thunder and lightning shake the ground. People are rushing to seek cover from the storm.

Large hailstones and violent winds are destroying things all around.

Who on Earth could ruin such a beautiful day?
Well, it's Larry the Low; that's just his way.

Harry has seen enough!
He is circling back and answering
Larry's attack, pushing Larry
straight out of town!

By ushering in blue skies and sunshine, Harry is working hard to fix what Larrys' terrible weather tore down.

Larry is confused and very hurt by Harry's words. Larry doesn't mean to hurt or even ruin anyone's day. But it seems that is exactly what he often does.

Larry begins to believe that Harry is right, that he really sucks and that nobody likes him. He is very sad. He decides he will leave—so he flees far, far away.

Larry has now been gone for a very long time. Harry is giving everyone all of the sunshine that they can handle.

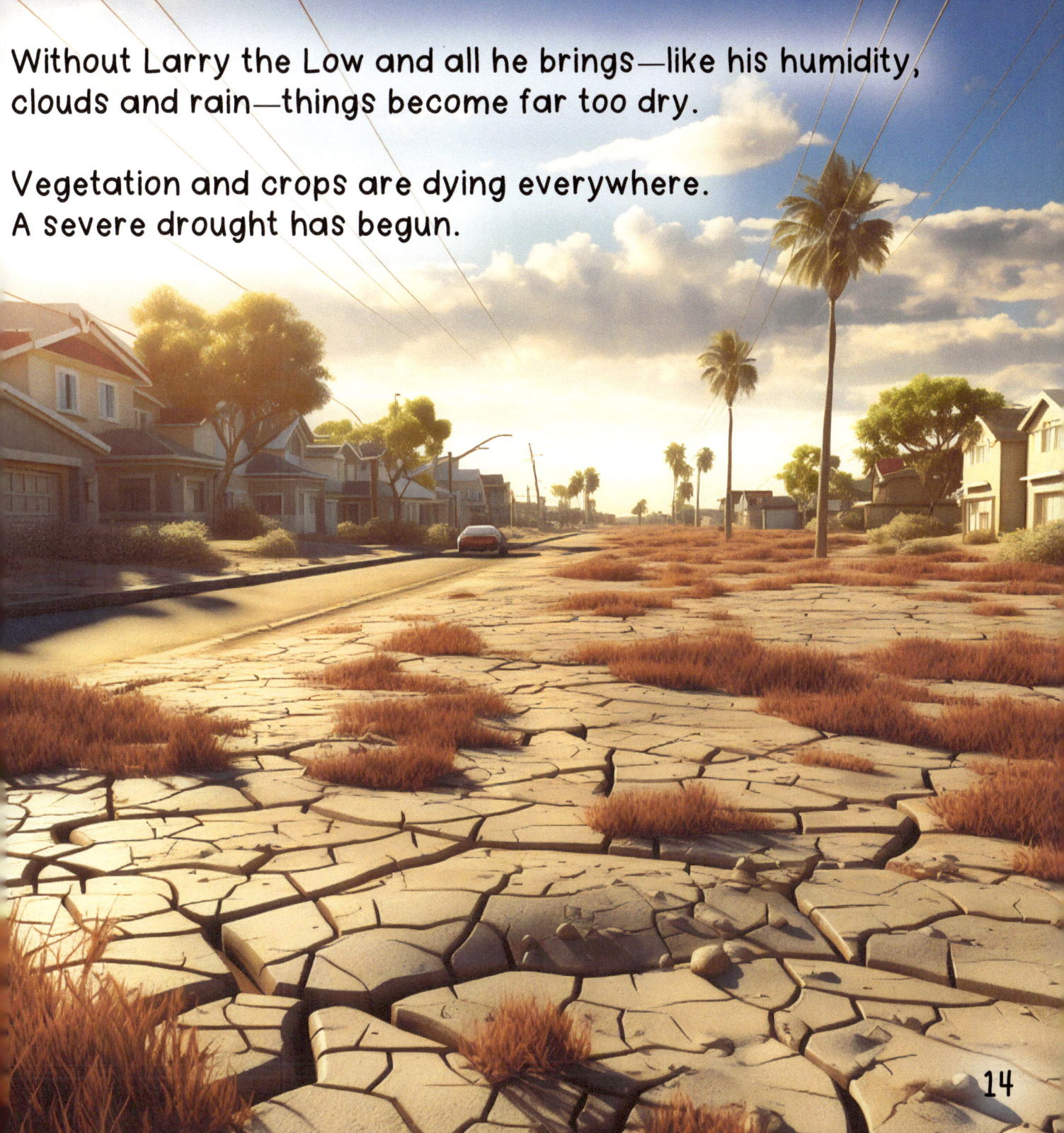

Without Larry the Low and all he brings—like his humidity, clouds and rain—things become far too dry.

Vegetation and crops are dying everywhere. A severe drought has begun.

Week after week go by with no Larry and no sign of rain. Harry the High has created a massive drought of Biblical proportions.

People around the world are suffering terribly as they pray for rain. They need water to drink. They need water for food. They need water for life. Soon, many people will begin to perish without the rain.

People have now grown tired of Harry the High's constant sunshine and insufferable heat. *Please let it rain*, they pray.

Mother Nature has now seen enough. She summons Harry the High and Larry the Low to her office for an emergency meeting.

"OK guys, what is the problem?" she asks with authority. Silence fills the room; both of them appear too scared to speak. "WELL! I want answers!" Mother Nature thunders.

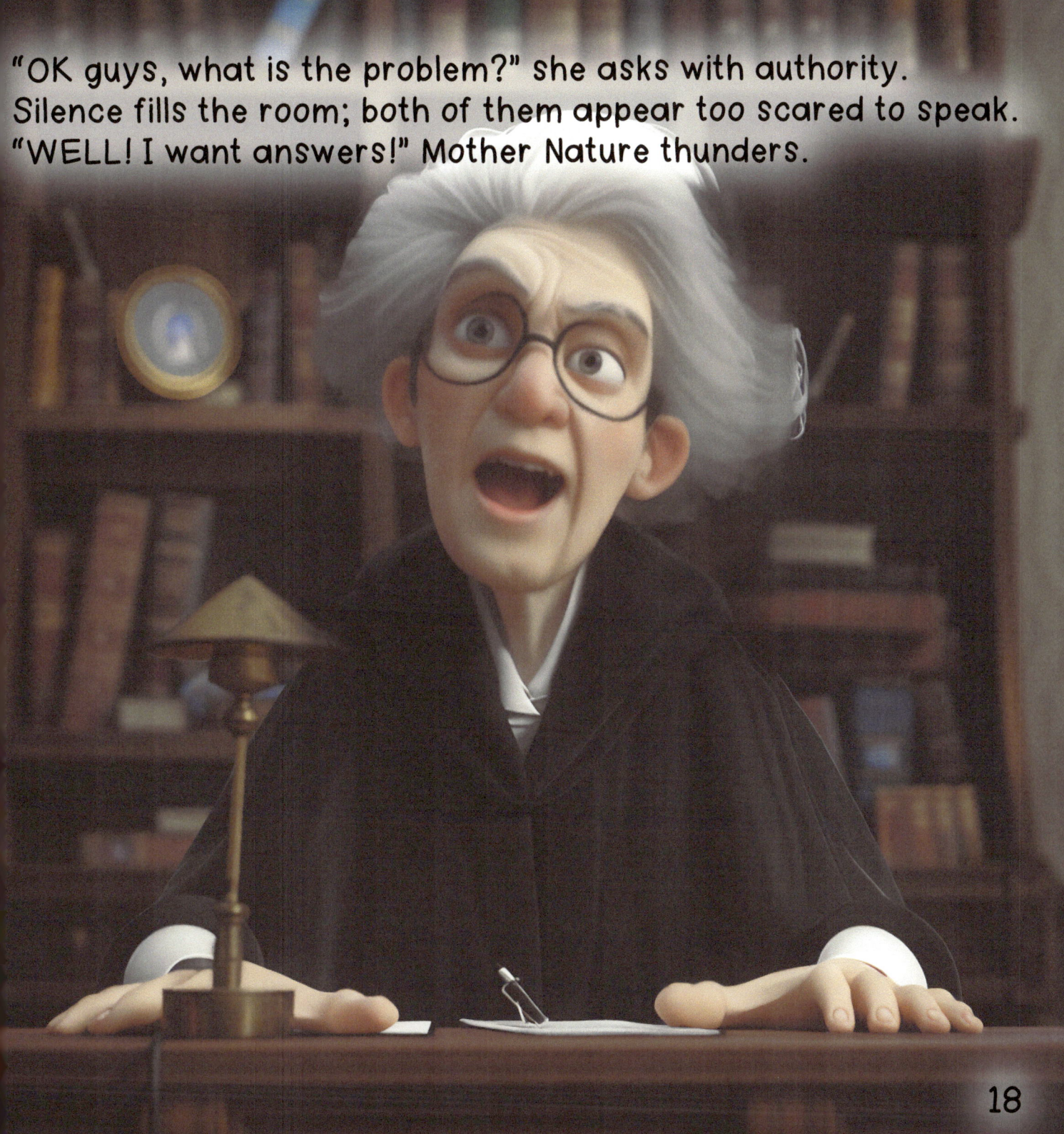

Very softly and with a nervous stutter, Harry begins to speak.

"I am very sorry, Madam. This is all my fault. I can't stop making sunshine. I am making everything way too dry and evaporating all of the water. All the plants are dying, and I am on the verge of killing everything!"

19

Mother Nature scolds Harry the High.

"Don't be silly, Harry. It IS your job to bring sunshine. It's Larry the Low's job to bring relief in the form of moisture, clouds, and rain. Where have you been, Larry? Why have you not brought any rain and allowed this terrible drought to occur?"

Unfazed by the lecture, Larry pouts, exclaiming, "I suck, I ruin pretty days and often destroy the things people value. Nobody wants me around."

Mother Nature is confused by Larry's attitude and his response. She asks Larry, "Why would you say such a thing?"

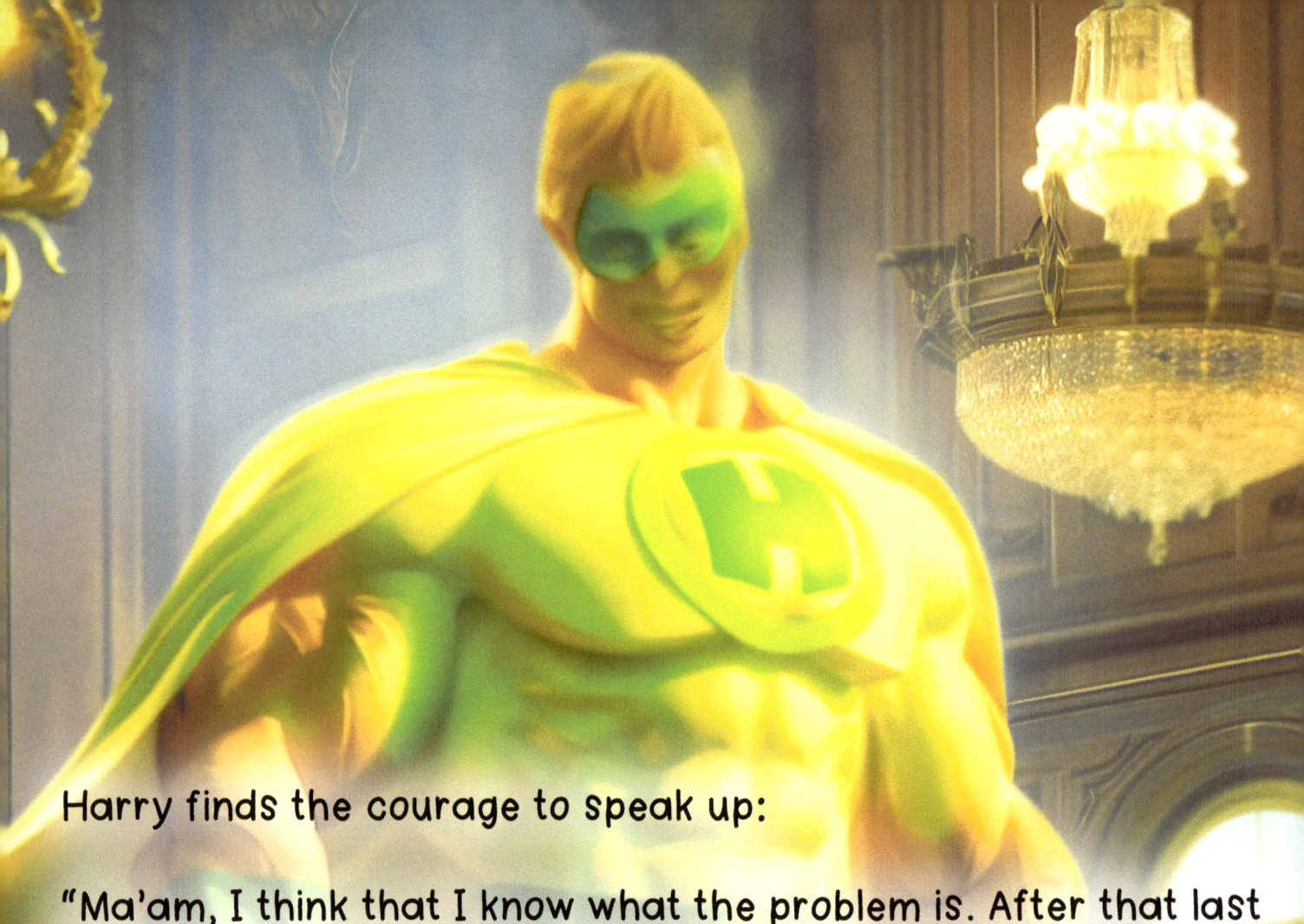

Harry finds the courage to speak up:

"Ma'am, I think that I know what the problem is. After that last big storm, I became very angry over all of the destruction. I blamed Larry for the people's suffering. I told him that nobody liked him, and that he should get lost forever."

Harry the High is very embarrassed over the hateful words he used towards Larry the Low. He never thought his words could have such a devastating effect.

Mother Nature is deeply saddened as she speaks:

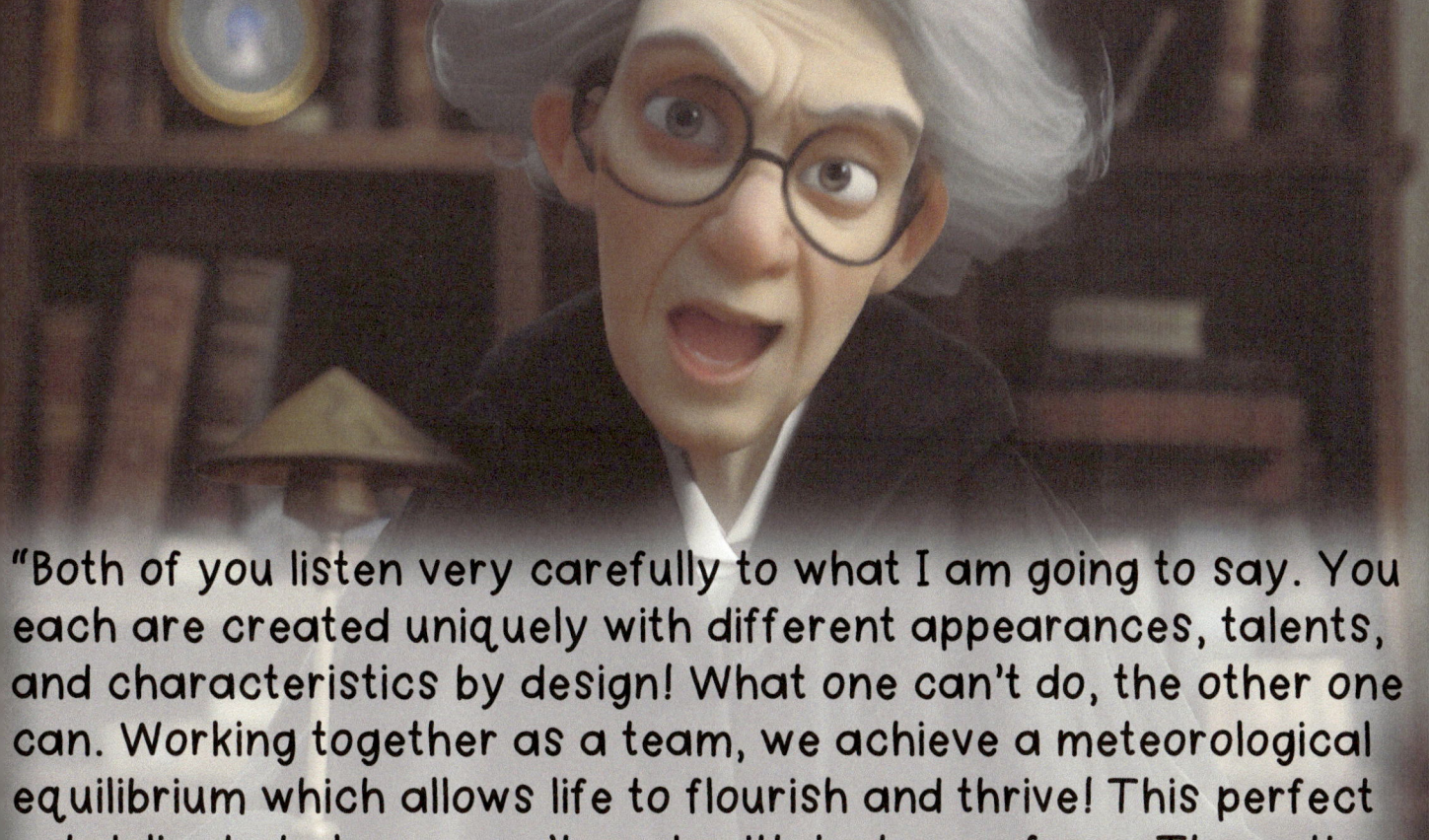

"Both of you listen very carefully to what I am going to say. You each are created uniquely with different appearances, talents, and characteristics by design! What one can't do, the other one can. Working together as a team, we achieve a meteorological equilibrium which allows life to flourish and thrive! This perfect yet delicate balance can't work with just one of you. The entire planet needs both of you! Do you understand me?"

Larry is excited about what he has just heard.
"So I don't suck! I DO have value! People need me too!"
he says with enthusiasm.

Harry is really ashamed over what his hateful words have done and understands what is needed in this situation...an apology. "Larry, I am so sorry for what I said. You are great! You are just as important as I am—we all understand that now! Please forgive me and be my friend again."

Realizing that they are both equally important and certainly needed, they hug one another and apologize for their squabble.

They promise to never forsake one another again. They agree to always work as a team in the future, bringing the world the weather it needs—even if it's not exactly what people always want.

About the Author

At a young age, Alan joined the United States Air Force and was placed in the weather career field. After only a year serving as a weather observer at Eglin AFB in Fort Walton Beach, FL, he was selected to be one of the first airman (E3) to attend the weather technician course (weather forecasting) at Chanute AFB in IL.

After serving honorably, Alan founded Weather One Corp with his best friend Mike. Weather One became one of the largest providers of aviation weather observations in the nation. As a prime contractor for the NWS and the FAA, Weather One provided service at over 50 airports. Their company was responsible for bringing the ASOS (automated surface observation system) online at the first commissioned location in Concordia, KS in 1995.

Alan has two daughters, one son and one granddaughter. He has coached basketball and softball teams as well as worked at the concession stand to help his children in their endeavors.

About Atmosphere Press

Atmosphere Press is an independent, full-service publisher for excellent books in all genres and for all audiences. Learn more about what we do at atmospherepress.com.

We encourage you to check out some of Atmosphere's latest releases, which are available at Amazon.com and via order from your local bookstore:

Yellow Yuba, by Jocelyn Tambascio
Alley: I Have Albinism, by Alethea Allen
Santa on a Surfboard, by Laura Sharp
Lilah Loves Life, by Brian Sullivan
The Christmas Witch, by Jaime Katusha
My Sister is Sick . . . What About Me?, by Mary Kay and Eli Olson
Yikes, I Saw a Barracuda!, by Tamara Anderson
Winston's Big Wind, by Barbara Reyelts
Twinkle Toes, by Connie Jameson
The Tail of a Trio, by Katherine Scott
Cow Days, by Christina Warfel
Logan and Lexi Meditate, by Denesia D. Rogers
Until We Meet Again, Leo, by Alexandra McGroarty

www.ingramcontent.com/pod-product-compliance
Ingram Content Group UK Ltd.
Pitfield, Milton Keynes, MK11 3LW, UK
UKHW050933250325
456677UK00008B/70